The Agile Edge

The Agile Edge

Managing Projects Effectively Using Agile Scrum

Brian Vanderjack, PMP, MBA
Principal Trainer PMHighway, LLC

BUSINESS EXPERT PRESS

The Agile Edge: Managing Projects Effectively Using Agile Scrum

First published in 2015 by
Business Expert Press, LLC
222 East 46th Street, New York, NY 10017
www.businessexpertpress.com

ISBN-13: 978-1-63157-186-2 (paperback)
ISBN-13: 978-1-63157-187-9 (e-book)

Business Expert Press Portfolio and Project Management

Collection ISSN: 2156-8189 (print)
Collection ISSN: 2156-8200 (electronic)

Cover and interior design by S4Carlisle Publishing Services
Private Ltd., Chennai, India

First edition: 2015

10 9 8 7 6 5 4 3 2 1

Printed in the United States of America.

Dedication

The following people played a role in moving this book's manuscript from draft copy to publishing ready: Lisa Clements, Nancy McMurry, Dr. Tim Kloppenborg, David Johnson, Hedrick Andrews, Michele Bowers, Matt Vanderjack, Mable Menard, Amy Olsen, Billie Morgan, Diane Rose Bolash, Mr. Rick DeJohn and Angela Lee. This book is also dedicated to my family: Terri, Matt, and Marc. My life would be empty without their love. Also, these people helped me grow into being an author: Dr. Omer Pamukcu, David Pells, Dr. Marty Burman, Paul Tedesco "Paul," and "Old Bill."

Those above contributed on their own behalf, and not in association with any organization. They did the good stuff. If there are any errors, that would be my doing.

Abtract

This concise book is an effective source for understanding Agile Scrum development; why we use it and how it works. It will explain to you how work gets done in manageable Iterations (AKA Sprints) and also the team meetings that keep work on track (AKA Ceremonies). Also, since risk is a constant threat to any team based project, managing risk in an Agile Scrum environment is specifically discussed.

Therefore, this book is for you as a:

- New Agile Scrum team member, this book will help you get up to speed quickly
- Team leader this book describes the foundation of Agile Scrum so you can save time getting team members on the same page
- Trainer/Educator of Agile Scrum this book clearly defines Agile Scrum in a structured way so that students can learn how to effectively serve on an Agile team to improve their marketability

In short, if you need to know Agile Scrum, this book will show you how to own it.

Key words

Agile; Scrum; Agile Scrum; Iteration; Sprint; Visioning; Grooming; Back log; retrospective; project management; XP; Extreme Programming; Daily Standup; Retrospective; Burn down chart; Burn up chart; Rally; RTC; Application Life Cycle Manager; ALM; ALCM; Demo; Demonstration; Iteration; Spring; ScrumMaster; Scrum Master; Product Owner; continuous Integration; vision; Ceremony; Mission

Contents

Foreword

"Knowing how something originated often is the best clue to how it works."

—Terrence Deacon

Shortly after earning my MBA by going to night school, I was confronted with the first layoff at my company ever. And it was massive. Even though I was pretty sure I would get through unscathed, the remote chance of having to explain to my family that I was jobless seared the unpleasant thought of that possibility into my mind forever. Fortunately, I was spared. But I came to the realization that I needed a skill that was portable between companies and industries. My second realization was that "you are only as valuable to your current company as you are to someone else." So after much thought, I picked a career and worked my way into project management and leading projects. This role was hard work for me and I knew that there had to be a better way to get all the stuff done. What annoyed me no end was that a bright acquaintance of mine, Jane, would often show off a how-to booklet she had written on how to do projects, but had never shared even when I asked about it. But then, a miracle occurred that would soon put me on a new and exciting path.

Around this time, a new contractor named Paul arrived on our floor in a high-rise building in the heart of downtown Chicago. I had the chance to see his resume. Clearly, Paul was a battle-seasoned, dyed-in-the-wool, project manager. In fact, he had published some of his ideas and was even interviewed by one of the two best-known Chicago newspapers on his unique, successful vision. By vision, I mean his interpretation of what the future should look like. One day, he asked me if I wanted to get better at getting projects into production better, faster, and cheaper. To that offer I gladly accepted. He took on responsibility for being my coach. Once I gradually got to trust his methods, and used them, my in-flight projects, which we were using as an experiential-lab/testing-ground, were getting done so well that it was rare to get any backlash from implementations. As I understood Paul's method more and more, I was able to apply his day-to-day teachings for many years to come as they were practical and intuitive. Before long, I had settled into a successful 15-year stint as Project Manager, at the large, well-known telecom firm. Honestly, managing projects had become pretty easy (Well, passing those challenging project audits, where the "right" method changed monthly, was always a challenge for me). Due to my friend Paul, I now had that portable, marketable skill; that of effective project management. And, I have no need to look at Jane's magic project-booklet, because my intuition tells me that the stuff that Paul taught me and how my understanding of it evolved over the years make Jane's booklet less than useless to me now (no, that is not her real name).

Soon after, I began to feel a responsibility to pay forward Paul's favor to others who needed similar assistance. Plus, I had vowed never to be a "Jane." After much consideration, I crafted my vision statement to personally address the dislocated, or potentially dislocated professionals; "Sharing with professionals the job skills that improve their ability to remain gainfully employed, and provide those skills so that they can take them to their next career as their current skills age out." To implement this, I teach college courses in my free time on team building, communication, project management, risk management etc. My vision leads me to meet very interesting, often brilliant people, develop new skills, and has provided interesting recognitions along the way, though I must admit that the Chicago Tribune has not interviewed me yet (smile!). My vision has moved me into creating this book with the intent of sharing the "how to" of Agile Scrum so that others can partake in the rewards that people who are good at Agile have been experiencing. What I have noticed is that Agile Scrum is similar in many ways to the style of team leadership that Paul taught me many years ago. I suspect that is why learning this has felt so natural to me.

As for the path forward, I will break down the process of Agile Scrum in the same way Paul had broken down Project Management for me years ago.

Although after reading this book some project managers may feel that AgileScrumMasters will get to replace them, this is not the case.

When a project effort must complete all requirements, there is significant risk to the performing organization or stakeholder community, each requirement must be explicitly captured, and/or it is necessary to have all in-scope items approved by many, then classical project management definitely has a place. That is, there are some projects that will work best with project management methodologies.

While writing this, I have made an intentional effort to integrate the jargon of our Agile culture into the lexicon used for this book. I am a firm believer that once you have an intimate understanding of the words used in a process to the point you can effectively speak them yourself, then understanding the process is orders of magnitude easier. My goal for this book is that it will leave you in a better position in your career as you learn how to enact change in an organization. And in using this awesome new methodology, you will be achieving outstanding results through team collaboration. My second desire is that you, through what is presented in this book, and through your experiences trying out what you learn here, will be in a solid position to share this knowledge with others. I suspect you will enjoy your Agile journey and I am excited to share with you the body of knowledge that makes it a pleasure for me to start my work day.

Brian Vanderjack, PMP, MBA
Agile Coach—For the Best Telecom in the World
Principal Trainer—PMHighway LLC
Brian@PMHighway.com

Disclaimer

Readability Tips

Many books use the word "**Sprint**" rather than "**Iteration**." Some people actually think that the words are interchangeable. However, to perform at a "Sprint Level" pace is decidedly NOT sustainable. Rather, in **Agile Scrum** we like to work at a "sustainable pace." That is, "Sprints" are not sustainable; they are short bursts of high energy and should certainly NOT be a way of life out of respect for people and their families.

All words specific to **Agile** are capitalized and bolded when first used, and capitalized thereon. When an **Agile** term refers to an individual or collective of individuals, the words are squished together, as well as capitalized. For example: "**AgileScrumTeam**," "**ProductOwner**," "**ScrumMaster**," "**BuildTeam**" etc.

A key to learning a new professional skill is to understand the jargon of that industry. To assist you in learning the jargon of Agile Scrum, a **Glossary** of common Agile Scrum terms is included at the end of this book.

CHAPTER 1

A Fast Look at an Agile Scrum Project

Success "come(s) only from continuous effort ... "

Napoleon Hill

Chapter Purpose

As an Agile Coach, Agile practitioner, and Agile evangelist
I want to provide a high-level explanation of Agile Scrum methodology
So that readers have a basic understanding of this methodology, and this can lay a foundation for the rest of this book.

Comment: *The above is in the format of a **User Story**. User Stories are very similar to a sentence in a **requirements** document. They will be discussed in detail later in this book.*

Why Agile Scrum is Valuable

Agile Scrum is a process that is used by many companies you would have heard of to guide the creation and delivery of working software to the client community. It is also utilized in many other areas; for example, in creating online training. To me, the top reasons as to why Agile Scrum is well-liked by end users, clients, customers, and organizational leadership are:

- That every 2 to 4 weeks a Retrospective takes place, so the team can continually improve on its ability to perform.
- Requirements (called **User Stories**) are prioritized, so important features can be delivered to production; fast and first.
- In Agile, a midstream project change request is no harder to process than an initial requirement. This is a key reason why the **DevelopmentTeam** and **TestTeam** have no issues with midstream alterations in scope.

- Learning and growth are expected, meaning people have no fear of trying out new or different methods and potentially failing. In fact, agile teams prefer to "fail fast" so that they get to know what they need to confront as soon in the project's life as possible.
- Agile teams work closely with the **ProductOwner** as requirements are created. Then, ProductOwner inspects the work-product regularly to confirm what they really want.
- Agile has become the methodology of choice for getting work completed in a number of large, well-respected companies.
- It is my experience that **ScrumMasters**, at this moment in time, are more marketable than those with only classical project management skillsets detailed on their resumes.

As for the reason why Agile is valuable to me, once I learned enough about Agile Scrum to realize that it was a superior method of having project outputs better match customer expectations, I was hooked.

Formulating an Example Agile Scrum Project

On November 18, 2014, just before Thanksgiving, a fire started in my family's laundry room. The laundry room was destroyed by the fire, and the rest of the house and its contents were ruined by smoke damage. Below, please find a picture of the fire damage to this room:

Our one-year old furnace

This pipe was the gas pipe for the water heater. You don't see the water heater as the firemen tossed it out the window -wow!

All documents in fire safe were fine, even though the room got so hot the silver solder metal that held our water pipes together melted. I was lucky to get it open as the plastic parts on its face melted.

As we had practiced fire drills for years when the kids were young, the entire family was outside within moments of my wife, luckily, noticing the fire. The most stressful call I have ever made in my life was the first of dozens of calls to our insurance company. This first call was simply: *are we insured?* You see, insurance is easy to overlook, until a risk manifests itself as an event. They responded, "Yes, you are insured." A sense of relief overtook me.

The insurance adjuster arrived at our home the next day, and she confirmed again that we were covered; however, it would be close as to what was insured versus what we would have to pay. She then asked her best cleanup crew and contractor for fixed bids.

The house was vacant for a few weeks while the fixed bids were created. When the estimates came in, the bottom line was that everything was covered except for the family room.

As I have had many years of experience in project management, including a real-estate build-out project (I usually lead IT projects, but, the skills of doing projects is portable between industries), and have a lifetime of experience doing DIY (do it yourself) projects in my home, I took on the role of General Contractor. Now the real story begins; how the project would run in an Agile Scrum environment.

IT Industry Background

About 15 years ago, Waterfall was the mainstay development methodology that companies used for many years to manage projects. That is, when a project was first started, the team would know (in their unique way) when the entire effort was due and almost exactly what they were creating; from the beginning. If a change was needed after a project team was launched, any change required a miniature project to run concurrent with the main effort called a change request. When I worked during this period, all team members had to reapprove everything! That took forever! Then fortunately, many well-known people in the IT industry met face-to-face in 2002 and created the AgileManifesto.org. They created a blending of the best of breed techniques from various methodologies known at the turn of the century. However, the idea of bringing all this great stuff under one umbrella is huge. And when you consider that key members in the IT space actually agreed on anything, this is truly amazing.

To see the stunningly excellent and simple foundation of Agile, just look below:

Manifesto for Agile Software Development

We are uncovering better ways of developing
software by doing it and helping others do it.
Through this work we have come to value:

Individuals and interactions over processes and tools.
Working software over comprehensive documentation.
Customer collaboration over contract negotiation.
Responding to change over following a plan.

That is, while there is value in the items on the right, we value the items on the left more.

Kent Beck	James Grenning	Robert C. Martin
Mike Beedle	Jim Highsmith	Steve Mellor
Arie van Bennekum	Andrew Hunt	Ken Schwaber
Alistair Cockburn	Ron Jeffries	Jeff Sutherland
Ward Cunningham	Jon Kern	Dave Thomas
Martin Fowler	Brian Marick	

© 2001, the above authors
this declaration may be freely copied in any form,
but only in its entirety through this notice

(The Agile Alliance, 2001)

Example of Using Agile Scrum

So, let us begin with the working example of me redoing a family room which was ruined by the smoke from the fire, and the necessary efforts of the firefighters (800 gallons of water plus one entire wall destroyed!). The hands-on part **AgileScrumTeam**, that turns User Stories into physical elements of my home, is called the **BuildTeam**. The BuildTeam is composed of the DevelopmentTeam (they actually create the physical elements) and the TestTeam (they do the testing and quality inspections).

The entire area had to have its drywall ripped out, exposing the 2" × 4" wall studs and concrete floors, and 2" × 10" ceiling joists. Here are some assumptions:

- My wife, our ProductOwner, wants to have the living room restored to the "original" condition and has all the money needed.
- All supplies will be purchased at Home Depot.
- The team will be contractors working using fixed bid contracts. There will be one contract issued for each major User Story.
- A document called a Project Charter has been created for me by my wife as she wants us to not forget anything, and has documented her expectations (like having Pella windows) therein. It is a green-light-letter to get my project started and keep it going with the funds she has set aside for this restoral effort.

As for the roles: I am the ScrumMaster and my wife is the Product Owner. The DevelopmentTeam and the TestTeam will be the hired contractors.

Here is a picture of my family room, taken by my son on the day of the fire. Fortunately, our insurance covered the cleanup, and no one was hurt:

The desk on the left was my desk. Please notice the wall on the right. This wall was destroyed in moments by the firemen so that they could get access to the fire inside the walls. All the furniture was tossed about like it was weightless by the best fire-fighters from about five surrounding counties. By the way, there were 800 gallons of water used to put out the fire, meaning all the electronics (except my backup harddrive) were trashed. I had no idea these firemen knew how to toss a house about; a huge thanks again to each of them!

I will use the diagram immediately below as our map to using the Agile Scrum method in this chapter. Here is a roadmap of Agile Scrum:

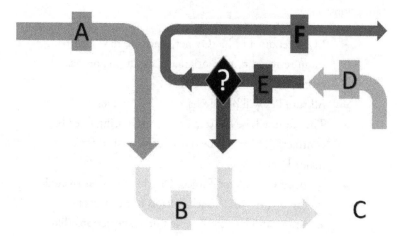

Now, let us start explaining the key points on the example above. Please note that the explanation in this chapter of the Agile Scrum process is at a high level only. A more detailed discussion is held in the later chapters.

A

ProductOwners write the requirements for the project in User Story format. This format is shown at the top of this chapter. Specifically, the **underscored and bold'ed** part is the template. When they are actually ready to write the User Stories out, this takes place with the help of the ScrumMaster and BuildTeam during a **Vision Ceremony.**

The team also needs metadata to be attached to the User Story for it to be useful. If you look at User Story CH1 #2, you will find some example metadata attached to that User Story:

- Estimated duration in Story Point format (we will get into Story Points later).
- The key to the User Story it decomposes and keys to any user stories that decompose it.
- A list of any assumptions or risks.
- Etc.

Please find below a handful of example User Stories for the project at hand:

1.

Epic User Story

As a mother, home owner, ProductOwner, and as supreme ruler of the house,

I want my family room restored to its original prefire state

So that I can enjoy the room's facilities again, as we did before the fire.

Example uses of User Story Examples:

1.1.

User Story ID: CH1 #1

As the ProductOwner,

I want to contract out the hard wood flooring,

So that that we have a human friendly surface to walk on.

1.2.

User Story ID: CH1 #2

As the ProductOwner,

I want to contract out all aspects of the windows, including treatments,

So that the windows look nice and the rays of the sun can be reduced or virtually eliminated.

> 1.2.1 Metadata for Use Story Ch1 #2: Assumptions and Details
>> 1.2.1.1 We assume the windows are replaced before we start our project
>> 1.2.1.2 We will have thermal pane windows with UV protection
>> 1.2.1.3 We will use Pella brand windows.
> 1.2.2 Story Point Value: 13 (Story Points are a high-level estimate of duration, assigned by the BuildTeam; this is covered in detail in Chapter 4)
> 1.2.3 Priority: 1 (Priority is set by the ProductOwner, who understands the business' prioritization schema.)

...

1.3

User Story ID: CH1 #7

As the ProductOwner,

I want safety items added like smoke detectors and fire extinguishers,

So that that we have a safer home.

Please note that metadata was added to CH1 #2 (only) during a Grooming Ceremony. In Chapter 3, metadata will be discussed in full. Also, this Agile Ceremony is very similar to the Initiating process group at the Project Level (PMBOK, p. 69).

B

"B" is the Iteration Planning Ceremony. At this time, the Backlog is populated with prioritized User Stories; the User Stories are sorted based on Priority. The idea is that the BuildTeam takes ownership of User Stories from the backlog. They take the one with the highest priority first.

In the case of our example, the User Story with a priority of 1 is the one that will be worked first; installation of windows. Since this will keep the weather out, it appears this one makes for a great first one to work on.

Also at this time, once a User Story is selected to be worked on, Tasks are created. These Tasks are to hold the information that is needed to create the work-product the task is referring to.

C

In this section of the process, we create detail-designs and code. Once coding is done, user testing is then undertaken. These aforementioned items are the work of the DevelopmentTeam.

While this is going on, the TestTeam creates test conditions and stores them in a Task.

So, to continue the project, this is where windows and window treatments are installed. Also, we will look for the contractor to build a checklist of tests, and will provide proof that the tests were done, and the tests passed.

D

If the TestTeam will execute any Test Plans that are scheduled with respect to any work outside the immediate area that is being worked on. This includes testing like if the windows match the windows upstairs.

E

This is where the Demonstration to the ProductOwner occurs. If there are any User Stories in the iteration that were not previously approved, this is the last chance to have them approved for the current iteration. Approved User Stories in this book are called "Done."

In this case, my wife the ProductOwner checks out the contractor's work. And she said all was good.

IF

There are no more User Stories for this project, or the funds run out, or some other reason to stop working on the project....we exit

ELSE

do another iteration.

F

This is where the code for the project is considered "Done." Once it is ready for end users to use in their day-to-day business processes, it is considered "Done–Done."

In the case of our project, the move to production blends nicely with the move-back-in date.

Summary

In this chapter, we took a fast, high-level look at Agile Scrum. This was done to lay a foundation for the remaining chapters.

Knowledge Reinforcement

1. In your company, do the requirements owners play an active role in the project's progress after the initial requirements are approved? If not, how would you go about getting more of the attention of the ProductOwner?

2. The (controversial) Hawthorne Effect indicates that the more the attention given to employees, the harder they will work. During which ceremonies are individuals most likely to show off their work and get attention? And if so, can just scheduling a ceremony increase the likelihood of tasks completing on time as promised?

3. (In Class Activity) The ScrumMaster is like a parent to the team. What characteristic would you look for in a ScrumMaster? Would you expect them to solve every issue and/or problem?

4. (In Class Activity) Assume that you are a general contractor asked to re-do a kitchen. Please create at least five User Stories to support this effort. Please add some metadata to one of your new User Stories.

Reference

The Agile Alliance (2001). "Manifesto for Agile Software Development", AgileManifesto.org.

CHAPTER 2

How Agile Scrum Works

"Innovation distinguishes leaders from followers."

Steve Jobs

Chapter Purpose

As an AgileScrumCoach and Agile practitioner,
I will explain the Agile Methodology's Life cycle,
So that people who want to understand the detail in the steps in the Agile Scrum at a deeper, richer level, can.

Introduction

First, a Ceremony in Agile Scrum is a meeting that is re-occurring, and has a specific purpose. Each ceremony will be discussed in detail in Chapter 3. One aspect of Agile Scrum I personally found confusing while learning Agile Scrum was that I began my journey with a misconception that every aspect of the Agile Scrum process was iterative. As I learned more, I began to realize that there are actually three parts that compose Agile Scrum. The first two below take place on demand, and the last, the "iteration," is repetitive:

- Visioning
- Grooming
- Iteration

The above three items are discussed below.

Vision Ceremony

The Visioning Ceremony is where the ProductOwner works with the selected members of the Scrum team to capture and refine what is requested. Once the requirement is well understood, the ProductOwner, with the assistance of the team creates a User Story in the correct format (demonstrated at the top of this chapter). What the team needs from the Product Owner before this takes place is for the ProductOwner to explore the needs of all relevant stakeholders and then bring those "asks" forth to the Vision Ceremony.

Organizational Vision is important for the ProductOwner to understand. The purpose and soul of an organization is to strive to fulfill their **Vision**. The Vision identifies strategic, long-term direction. It defines what the organization should invest effort into, and, acts as a filter to sift out activities that are not within scope. If you look on the Internet, you will notice larger companies post these on their websites. Vision Statements are captured in writing after careful discussions between the leaders of the organization. The vision is important, as if an AgileScrumTeam aligns itself with the organization's vision, it will necessarily choose to invest time and resources into the types of activities the organization has been carefully constructed to profit from. A short way to think of what a vision statement does is, it defines what is in and out of scope for the organization. The vision is not the only selection criteria to apply to prospective opportunities, but it should be the first filter. Below, please find a brief process map that covers the Visioning. Visioning is the process of creating requirements for the BuildTeam, where the build team is a sub-team of the AgileScrumTeam, and includes the developers and testers of the Agile Scrum team.

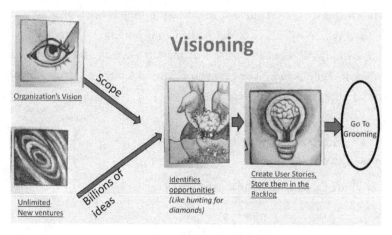

- Legal Mandates: Many governmental agencies have an interest in how organizations execute business practices on a day-to-day basis. Be it from not dumping toxic waste into fresh drinking water, not releasing GMOs into our fragile environment, or even following prudent financial measures as spelled out by Sarbanes-Oxley. Legal mandates can be extremely costly if not addressed.

- Executive Pet Projects: Executives have a high-level understanding of what needs to get done. This is because they have access to incredible amounts of well-organized material that their staff provides, and, input from the various nonwork-related organizations they belong to, and often lead. Occasionally, they will launch their own effort that sometimes looks rather bizarre. But, what I have found is that executives get those leadership roles by being smart, and I have also found that once time goes by, executive initiatives start to make sense.

- Innovations: An innovation that will soon play a big role in our lives is the 3D printer. I assume that since it can shoot out live cells, I want to eventually be able to tell a printer to make me a hamburger or pizza. Off the top of my head, the first project I would undertake if I were a factory owner is to identify all factory machine components that can be made on a 3D printer, and which ones would be the best to produce in-house. This would certainly be an example of an effort driven by technology improvements.

- Industry Trends: There is a trend in the airlines industry to rely on finding "black boxes" after a plane goes down. Eventually, the idea of information primarily being stored entirely on the "Black Box" will be eliminated, as the airlines will start storing detailed flight information on the cloud. This could also allow for a detailed analysis of all flights real time, so that even seemingly successful flights could be inspected before they land, or just plain fall out of the sky. Therefore, assuming this look into the future is correct, many airlines would implement this industry trend as it would fall into the notion of Industry Trends.

- Public Good: Some projects are done simply because it is the right thing to do. For example, a company might buy up a few hundred acres of tropical forest in South America to offset their carbon emissions. A project here could be to set up a post to monitor the forest to ensure that it remains healthy and alive.

- Competitive Pressure: Let us say Burger King's nearest competitor starts selling gourmet coffee at rock-bottom prices. And further assume that Burger King's experts indicate that it will take years to catch up and employ the competitor's model. My knee-jerk reaction is to try to dwarf the competition by inviting Starbucks to have a space in key locations. This effort is to bring Starbucks in to select Burger King restaurants. This imagined scenario would be an excellent example of reacting to competitive pressure.

- Risk: This is when there is a possibility that the expected outcome will not match the actual result. Typically, when working on efforts, we focus on the impacts of adverse events. Please see the chapter on Risk for more information on dealing with adverse risk events. I feel obligated to tell you that if your entire AgileScrumTeam wins $600M in a lottery, this is an example of a positive risk event manifesting itself; at least "positive" from the team's perspective. One needs to have an idea of how to be ready for unimaginable events like this because occasionally they do happen.

- Defects: Algorithms are sequences of meaningful statements, that when executed produce a desired outcome. Defects are statements, or sets of statements, that result in undesired results when algorithms are being executed. What I often see happening is defects getting fixed once discovered, and all other work is set aside. I suggest that if one has a defect in the Agile world, if it can wait, the action to fix it should be addressed through creating a User Story. That way, the defect is prioritized against all other work that needs to get done.

- New Technology: For this one, look at the cell phone industry. Assume there is a new technology that allows a new cell phone apps. to hold memories for humans. I feel a valid assumption that students who need to pass tests would buy into this new technology, and if the activity is within the scope of the vision, it could make for an interesting game changer.

Select Opportunities

Once the universe of opportunities has been inspected to determine activities that pair well with the vision, an initial list of opportunities is created. Then based on how well the vision of the organization is met, specific opportunities will be selected to potentially be worked on, based on priority.

Create User Stories

The Productowner will then format the main ideas of potential projects into "Epic Level User Stories." Stories will be discussed in detail later, but for now, think of User Stories as a requirement that fits into a very simple, yet powerful template. The template has the items below to fill in:

1. "As a"
2. "I Want"
3. "So That"

Epic-level user stories are be **Decomposed** into much smaller User Stories that will be of more detail, but of a smaller estimated time commitment. The terminal event of decomposition is when User Stories are eventually broken up into "Tasks."

Backlog Grooming

Backlog grooming is the process of converting User Stories into a format that the BuildTeam is willing to accept into one of their Agile Scrum iterations. Please find below a short process map that outlines the Backlog Grooming process:

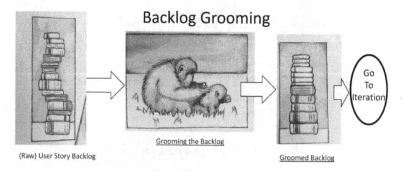

Backlog Grooming

(Raw) User Story Backlog   Grooming the Backlog   Groomed Backlog   Go To Iteration

The idea here is to transform the User Stories captured in the previous phase into User Stories that the BuildTeam can focus on. Here is another example of a User Story:

> **As a** big car manufacturer's president,
>
> **I will** ask our engineers to create a tire that stinks as bad as a skunk,
>
> **So that** if the young drivers ever go over 75 miles/hour, then the smell is let loose.

User Stories alone are not enough to get the job done. Metadata (information about other data), will eventually be added to User Stories to provide the needed detail.

Specifically with respect to the Grooming Ceremony, this is where the ProductOwner, ScrumMaster, and selected BuildTeam members review the User Story Backlog. Here is a list of activities during the Grooming Ceremony:

1. Confirm that new User Stories are formatted in User Story format, and also that they are written in a way that a typical reader can understand the intent of the person who originated the User Story.
2. Fill in the appropriate metadata for any new User Stories.
3. Apply "Story Point" estimates to each User Story (Story Points are similar to initial estimates in classic project management. Story Points will be further discussed in the next chapter).
4. Decompose into smaller User Stories any User Story that has too high an estimate. A "high estimate" is one that exceeds the maximum number of days that can reasonably be worked with-

in an iteration. The number of days in this context, to a classical project manager, is called **duration**. Please see Chapter 3 where "Story Points," which are an estimate of duration, are discussed.

The output of the User Story Backlog Grooming Ceremony is clean, and, tidy User Stories that fit the User Story format, that have Story Points applied to them.

Iterations

Of the three phases of the Agile Scrum Methodology, the Agile Scrum Cycle is truly where one begins to see the difference between just getting projects done, and, the Awesomeness of the Agile Scrum methodology. The following captures the main idea of the Agile Iteration Cycle:

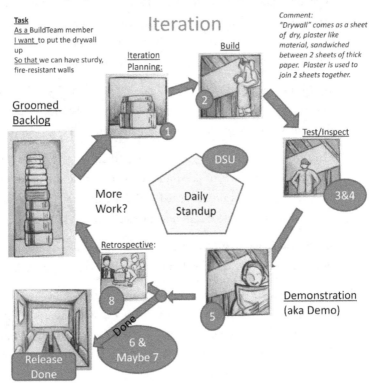

The Iteration Process is:

1. **Iteration Planning (Ceremony):** This is where the team picks User Stories, from a prioritized list, to work on. Once selected, they are considered committed to the iteration. In the case of the above illustration, the task to work on the drywall is selected to be worked on.

2. **Build:** This is where the Detail Design, code, and similar elements get created. Estimated hours are calculated by developers at the start of working on a User Story. The estimates are then stored in "Tasks." Tasks are like User Stories, but they are where work is done from, and they cannot be further decomposed. Before the Build phase is done, the developer is to unit test their work. For those of you with classical project management background, you mentally equate Tasks with "Work Packages" as found at the lowest level of the Work Breakdown Structure (WBS). Though not identical, work packages and Tasks are similar in that they represent the most decomposed effort and house metadata.

    In this case, a member of the BuildTeam went to Home Depot and purchased some drywall and necessary tools and supplies. They then did the work to install the drywall.

    Unit Test: Developers typically inspect their own code for defects through the use of previously created test cases embedded in User Stories. More advanced Agile Scrum teams will have software to determine if the code meets all known standards.

    In this case, the drywall worker looks closely at all the seams to make sure that the seams will not show after paint is applied.

3. **Environment Test:** This is when testing takes place beyond one module of code. Some examples are system testing, iteration testing, one-up/one-down testing, regression testing, etc. The TestTeam will test multiple applications together to make sure that they "talk" to each other as expected. This is becoming increasingly more mechanized. The real work for the TestTeam at this time is creating effective and efficient test conditions and/or

acceptance criteria. More advanced shops will rely on mechanical processes to execute these kinds of tests.

With respect to rebuilding the family room, the areas that the workers were in are inspected to make sure no tools are left behind, and that there is no mess.

4. **Demo** (Ceremony): The Demo (short for "Demonstration") is the time that the AgileScrumTeam demonstrates its excellence to the ProductOwner, in a bundle, rather than in parts. To explain, when exercising "continuous delivery" the ProductOwner will only see a small chunk of the iteration's work-product at a time. The Demo is when all deliverables for an iteration are put on display for the ProductOwner at the same time. In the human mind, if something is displayed in a different way (in this case, seeing the entire work-product for the iteration, rather than one component at a time), perceptual expectations can be deadened, and, the ProductOwner can occasionally look at the bundled work-product in a new light. This means, they will have fuel to create more ideas to convert into valuable UserStories.

    For the example, the drywall is inspected by the mother of the house to make sure there are no holes, and that the drywall pieces are attached to each other in a way that they look seamless.

5. **Done:** This is when the TestTeam declares the code to be working to the specifications laid down by the Test Cases and/or acceptance criteria. "Done" is a term that each ScrumTeam should create a definition for as teams usually have their own definition of Done. This team-specific definition of done should be stored in the team's Social Contract. To explain, a "Social Contract" is very similar to what Waterfall calls a Project Charter. It contains answers to how an AgileScrumTeam will manage itself.

    Our definition of Done, in this case, is when the test cases are successfully addressed, and the mother of the home approves the deliverable.

6. **Move to Production:** Whenever it makes business sense, and it is safe to do so, code is to be moved into production when it is ready. In practice, it is often wise to target a certain date for releasing code so that everyone outside the AgileScrumTeam who will be impacted by new features and functionality can plan for the arrival of the newest version of the application.

   When defects are found in production, under classical project management, there is often a "warrantee" period. When defects are found during this warrantee period, they get fixed with no-charge billed back to the paying customer. In Agile, we recognize that if you pull people off development to work defects, you will reduce the about of new functionality in the next release. So, in Agile, we may have a warrantee period, but it will be structured in a way that defects are to be converted to User Stories, and only worked when they have enough priority to get worked on (as assigned by the ProductOwner, with the assistance of the AgileScrumTeam).

   An example of moving this idea to production is allowing limited use of the family room as it now has walls!

   Comment: Defects found during an iteration are fixed as part of the normal Aglie Scrum process. If a defect is found after the iteration, it becomes a story and prioritized as part of the product backlog.

7. **Retrospective:** This is where the entire team meets and determines what went well and what areas need to be improved. As Agile supports a "Fail fast" mentality, people are not to be shy about making a mistake. Rather, they realize that most mistakes are a manifestation of poor process. So, mistakes are called out (but not by person). Once the list of improvements is created, the team examines the list to determine if the stuff that went right can be duplicated or expanded. They also look at what went wrong. The team then decides what is realistic to fix, and once determined, User Stories are added to the User Story Backlog.

This is a great time to buy some pizza and sit on the floor of the newly drywalled room. During the conversation, all people involved in the project identify what went right, and what can be improved the next time. In this case, all agree that the drywall went up fast and neat! Dust from sanding the drywall was noted in some areas. The team notes this in a log, and they decide to hire someone from Service Master (this company cleans up spaces) next time for cleanup as they get the point that drywall installers may not be the best choice for a great cleanup job.

8. **Release Complete:** If there is no reason to perform another iteration, or, funding runs out for the effort at hand, or all the work is complete, then the Done work is migrated into production. Once work is moved into production, it is called "Done–Done."

There is one more critical ceremony yet to be discussed. It takes place each working day. It is called the **Daily Standup:** The daily standup takes place each day. Only people on the immediate Agile Scrum Team are allowed to speak. The agenda of this call is…

A. What is the Burn down Chart telling us? (covered in Chapter 3)
B. Status by Agile Team Member (Each person is given 2 minutes or less to speak)

    1) What did I do yesterday?
    2) What will I do today?
    3) Do I have any impediments?
    4) Have I updated my hours in the ALCM?

Comment: ALCM stands for Application Life Cycle **Management**. It is where all information regarding Agile Scrum projects is stored. It also provides transparency into the health of the AgileScrumTeam and its progress by any interested, authorized stakeholder.

In the case of this effort, the team meets daily for the life of the effort to bring the family room up to speed. While drywall is being installed, the person doing the drywall answers the four questions above.

Summary

In this chapter, we took a good look at the process side of the Agile Scrum Methodology. In the next paragraph, we will look at the various systems that keep this process moving and effective.

Knowledge Reinforcement

1. (Team Project) One night, a chimpanzee named Playful Imp escaped from Brookfield Zoo, in Illinois. Apparently he hid in the baggage compartment of a Mega Bus, and right by your house is where he finally figured out how to escape the luggage compartment under the bus. As it was a nice late spring day, and the temperatures were perfect, you left a few windows of your home open; much to Playful Imp's delight. As if guided by radar, he quickly finds your hobby room, and utterly destroys all the gadgets, tools, instructions, supplies, etc. that you need to do your hobby. By the time the Playful Imp is brought back to the zoo, there is nothing of use or value in your hobby room any more. Please answer these questions:

   a) Identify one of your personal hobbies. Assume it was your house that Playful Imp invaded. Please write the User Story to let all stakeholders know you are working on restoring all the materials in your hobby room. This is referred to as an "Epic" user story.

   b) The master User Story is called an Epic. It defines the entire work effort as if written in a Project Charter in classical project management. Epics are decomposed just like organization charts are broken down into finer granularity. Please write two to four User Stories that would be a good decomposition of the Epic story. For those of you with a classic project management background, this is an identical thought process to decomposing the WBS. Please do not feel obligated to identify all the children; just enough to get started understanding the format of a User Story.

    c) Identify the metadata for one of the child User Stories. A child User Story decomposes the User Story that it is subordinate to.

2. (Class Project) It has come to my friend's 23-year-old daughter's attention that there is snow and ice landing in Texas during the winter! Her idea is to buy a 4-wheel-drive truck and snow plow, and contract with the elite in Texas to keep their streets clear of snow and shovel their driveways. That will keep the snow and ice from bothering these busy, rich people.

    a) Please create a vision statement for this business idea.

    b) What would the Epic level User Story look like?

    c) Create at least four User Stories under the Epic User Story that will help her understand the work that she is going to do.

3. (Team Experience) Identify a hobby that interests you and your team, specifically something that takes at least half-dozen specific tasks to create. Once your team identifies a hobby that is agreeable, please capture the following in a method that works for your learning environment (e.g., PowerPoint, Prezi, poster board, white board, etc.) where your in-class work-product can be shared. *Please note, you will not actually do this hobby*, rather we are going to work on establishing the infrastructure to work on this effort. Please capture the following:

    a) In plain English, what is the hobby you are choosing to work on as a team?

    b) In plain English, what are the inputs, processes, and outputs of the effort you will work on as a team for this exercise?

    c) What is the Epic level story to capture the essence of the hobby activity your team is about to explore? As a reminder, the format of a User Story uses the template: "As a"...."I want"... "so that." Also, and Epic level User Story is just like any other User Story except it is expected that the Epic Level User Story will be Decomposed, and it represents an entire effort, not a segment of an effort.

    d) Decompose the Epic User Story into three User Stories. Please display your three User Stories that are components of the Epic that visually shows them as a part of the Epic.

Ways to do this could look like an organization chart, a mind web, or even an outline format.

e) In order to get experience of a Grooming Ceremony a team, present your results to the entire class. Update your User Stories with their suggestions as appropriate.

4. In your company, do the requirements owners play an active role in the project's progress after the initial requirements are approved? If not, how would you go about getting more of the attention of the ProductOwner?

CHAPTER 3

The System that Supports the Process

"If everyone is moving forward together, success will take care of itself."
Henry Ford

Chapter Purpose

As an Agile Coach and Agile Scrum Practitioner,
I will describe in detail the components of the Agile Scrum
Infrastructure. Specifically a deep dive will be taken into User Stories,
The Agile Tree Hierarchy, the AgileScrumTeam, Ceremonies, and the
Burn Down Chart
So that ScrumMasters, ProductOwners, DevelopmentTeam, and
TestTeam members can understand what the infrastructure is behind
Agile Scrum.

Introduction

What I have come to realize after years of using Agile Scrum is that
teams grow over time in the use of Agile Scrum. And as the teams ma-
ture, the more Agile Scrum processes they have in place, making them
even more effective. The key systems they all have in common are:

- User Stories
- Ceremonies
- Story Pointing
- Burn Down Chart

These three systems represent the minimum level of conceptual
knowledge needed to be effective in the use of Agile Scrum. Executing

well on these items is essential to seeing any benefit from Agile Scrum. So, please continue reading in order to understand these areas even more.

User Stories

Learning about User Stories is critical because they are the main component of Agile Scrum. No matter what you are doing on an Agile ScrumTeam, it all relates back to User Stories. Now that you know a bit about User Stories, here are some expectations User Stories should meet:

- They should facilitate the creation of a working code that meets the needs of a stakeholder, where the value of asked-for change is in excess of the investment.
- Convey information to the reader about what needs to get done, in the way it was meant by the writer to be interpreted
- Decomposed to the point where their estimated duration can fit within the time-box of an iteration.
- They are sufficiently descriptive to support the creation of test cases.

The template for User Stories, which the founders of Agile Scrum created, is brilliantly constructed. It is easy to learn, easy to remember, and forces a User Story creator to capture a well-carved slice of meaning from its parent User Story. But, just to be sure they accomplish their core function, User Stories should be reviewed by a peer to ensure, to the greatest extent, that the User Story conveys the intended meaning. And, before they are accepted into an iteration, the DevelopmentTeam and TestTeam need to agree that the User Stories are meaningful and complete.

Below, please find an explanation of the three parts of a User Story. I am doing this so that those who use User Stories can better understand how to be effective in writing and in using them:

As a

Describes the "who" is asking for the work to be done. This has three purposes;

- If the creator of the User Story is ever needed for consultation, it provides a clue to the home organization of the initiator.

- This part provides context for understanding what the person is asking for.
- It makes the creator focus on their perspective, or role, they are taking on when they create each User Story. That is, it forces the User Story writer to take on a specific perspective.

I want

The words "I want" steers the User Story writer to explicitly spell out what they have in mind. This "ask" is to be within the "scope" of the performing organization's vision statement, and the mission statement of the AgileScrumTeam. Another value to this is that it clearly calls out the work that is supposed to add business value.

So that

"So that" is the part of the template which describes the reason for the User Story, in terms of value-addition to the business. It can either be qualitative or quantitative. I feel this supports the creation of excellent test cases, test scripts, and acceptance criteria. Also, this will describe the end use of the User Story, which will further explain the use of the "I Want" part.

Please note that during iteration planning, the DevelopmentTeam and/or TestTeam should have the option of not picking up User Stories to work on if they are not useable. If defective User Stories are committed to and brought into an iteration, then they will likely destroy any cadence that the team has developed. And, this would also erode trust as the same ProductOwner who encouraged the team to accept incomplete User Stories will be the first to get mad at the team when it cannot deliver.

Ceremonies

Ceremonies are similar to meetings, but have a specific purpose based on which ceremony is being executed. Each has its own expected result, which does not change. Some ceremonies fall on specific days in the Agile cycle, and they are to be placed onto all ScrumTeamMember's Outlook calendars, and scheduled out for a very long time. This will eventually result in AgileScrumTeam members having this time marked out for the Ceremonies, and, they will from a habit behavior of getting ready and showing up, prepared.

As for when to hold the Ceremonies with respect to the Iteration cycle, I like to hold the Backlog Grooming and Iteration planning a few days before the Iteration starts. And then, holding the Demo and Retrospective on the last day of the iteration works quite well. The Daily Stand Up, and Parking Lot is to take place, without fail, once per business day; preferably at the start of the work day. All team members are expected to attend the Day Standup.

Please find below a chart that outlines how I like to schedule Ceremonies in relationship to an iteration. The assumption is that we are using a 2-week Iteration Cycle, starting on a Monday.

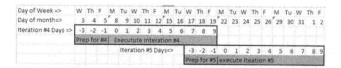

Day of Week	Iteration Day	Ceremonies for Current Iteration	Ceremonies for Next Iteration
Any	As needed	Vision	N/A
Wednesday	−3 (can also take place on demand)	Backlog Grooming	
Thursday	−2	Iteration Planning	N/A
Monday	1	Daily Standup + Parking Lot	N/A
Tuesday	2	Daily Standup + Parking Lot	N/A
Wednesday	3	Daily Standup + Parking Lot	N/A
Thursday	4	Daily Standup+ Parking Lot	N/A
Friday	5	Daily Standup (Halfway through the iteration+ Parking Lot	N/A
Monday	6	Daily Standup (Last Monday of Iteration) + Parking Lot	N/A
Tuesday	7	Daily Standup + Parking Lot	Start Backlog Grooming for next iteration Wrap up visioning for next Iteration
Wednesday	8	Daily Standup + Parking Lot,	Start Iteration Planning for next cycle

| Thursday | 9 | Daily Standup, Parking Lot, identify all User Stories for the Demo, and do a Dry run of the demo. EOD (End of Day) is the cut-off for approval of items in the Demo. | Continue Iteration Planning for next cycle |
| Friday | 10 | Daily Standup, Parking Lot, Retrospective, and Demo | Complete Iteration planning for next iteration |

Please find below a list of ceremonies and related information. As a friendly reminder, the more of these Ceremonies that are performed, and performed correctly, the more you will see the benefits of Agile Scrum:

Story Pointing

The idea of Story Pointing is to create, at a macro level, a rough planning estimate. The easiest way to explain Story Pointing is to assume that all participants in a Story Point meeting are co-located, and are in the same meeting room to create Story Points for User Stories. They are only allowed to estimate using the numbers 1, 2, 3, 5, 8, 13, 21, 34 … (for the mathematically inclined people reading this, this unusual number sequence is closely based on the Fibonacci sequence).

The team picks a well-understood User Story, of average duration. A Story Point of "8" is then associated with that average User Story, this is called the "pivot."

Then, the ScrumMaster shows the team a new User Story to estimate. Here is an exhibit of the numbers to apply Story Points to User stories:

How This One Relates to the Pivot (A Story Point of 8)	User Story's Story Point Value
Clearly larger than the pivot User Story	21 or 34 or higher
A little bigger than the pivot User Story	13
Pretty much the same as the pivot User Story	8
Somewhat smaller than the pivot User Story	5 or 3
A lot smaller than the pivot User Story, it would be rare to find a User Story for this effort less than this number.	1

Ceremony:	Purpose	Process/Agenda:	Who:	When:
Daily Standup	Establishes accountability for team members. Identify (but not discuss) issues and impediments.	Agenda: Each team member is to answer these four questions: 1. What I did yesterday? 2. What will I do today? 3. Do I have impediments? 4. Have I updated the ALCM?	The leader for this conversation is the ScrumMaster. The ScrumMaster, the Product Owner, the DevelopmentTeam, and the TestTeam are active participants. *Comment:* no one is to interrupt or add any words to someone's sharing time during the daily stand up. Extra content should be moved to the Parking Lot.	Daily, working days. This meeting is time-boxed to 15 minutes. A time-box is when a team is committed to starting and ending an activity at an agreed-upon time. *Comment:* these are never canceled or re-scheduled *Comment:* ScrumMaster should make note of anyone who provides the same status for a few days; if this happens, it is a signal that the person likely has an impediment.
Vision	Create User Stories	Agenda: ScrumMaster and selected team members assist ProductOwner in the creation of User Stories. *Comment:* This ceremony can be held at a time that works well with the iteration start and stop dates. It can also be scheduled on demand.	ProductOwner must attend. ScrumMaster, ProductOwner, and selected team members	Should be pre-scheduled weekly; however, these Ceremonies are on demand, based on ProductOwner's need to have UserStories created. *Comment:* If you preschedule this Ceremony (which is a good idea), it is OK cancel the upcoming meeting if you have nothing to discuss.
Iteration Planning	DevelopmentTeam and TestTeam members as for User Stories to work on in current iteration. 1. Work committed to during an iteration must not exceed the team's capacity. 2. When a BuildTeam member asks for work, they are committing to complete the User Story during the upcoming iteration.	Process: Input: Groomed, well written, User Stories that have a priority and Story Point estimate assigned. Process: BuildTeam selects User Stories to work on during the current iteration. As User Stories are selected, the BuildTeam members, and the persons taking the User Story are committed to doing the work. Output: BuildTeam has Usable User Stories to work on during the upcoming iteration *Comment:* if the Build Team cannot understand a User Story, it should be left on the Product Backlog	Leader: ScrumMaster Attendance: ScrumMaster, DevelopmentTeam and TestTeam. ProductOwner is optional.	This takes place at the beginning of an iteration.

Retrospective	Identify outcomes that were both good, and, topics that identify areas for improvement. *Comment:* Agile teams welcome improvement, and do not punish team members for mistakes. In Agile Scrum, we believe mistakes are a natural human activity, and excellent opportunities for learning and team growth. *Comment:* Realistically, at some point, if one person keeps making critical errors, the ScrumMaster should take corrective action.	**Process:** **Input:** All AgileScrumTeam members capture their relevant observations regarding lessons learned. These are shared at the retrospective. **Process:** 1. Positive and improvement comments are collected and captured in the ALCM (Agile Life Cycle Manager, a repository for all information needed to do the project) 2. Improvement items are captured in the ALCM 3. AgileScrumTeam determines which items it would like to tackle *Comment:* Do not put a name next to items collected at this meeting. The reality is that typically one identified issue signals that there are many involved. *Comment:* Activities identified by the team should be converted into User Stories and placed on the backlog.	The ScrumMaster should lead, and the entire AgileScrumTeam should participate.	Frequency; soon after every iteration.
Demo **(AKA Demonstration)**	The main purpose of the Demo is actually behavioral. It is to show off the work product of an Iteration to drive overall improvement so participants in success can receive accolades from the team.	**Process:** **Input:** Lists of improvements and successes achieved during the current iteration. **Process:** refine each time from the supplied list, and any new items that emerge at meeting time. Capture these items. Once capturing of items is complete, the team should identify which items should be converted into User Stories.	This is typically led by the ScrumMaster. I have heard of AgileScrumTeams that have their ProductOwner run the meeting (this is a good way to hold the interest of the ProductOwner, and keep them from multi-tasking during the Demo) To the greatest extent possible the entire AgileScrumTeam should be present to bask in the glory of a completed iteration.	1. A Demo should take place at least once per Iteration A Demo can take place on demand, especially if a complex User Story is to be inspected. However, these User Stories are to be shared again at Demo time.

Ceremony:	Purpose	Process/Agenda:	Who:	When:
	A secondary purpose is occasionally this meeting is to have the ProductOwner approve work products. However work products should be approved soon after they are finished. *Comment:* have you ever noticed that some people get more work done right before a status meeting (in any situation?) This is one reason the Demo is so effective.			
Parking Lot	Easy way for the team to meet, in a nonformal way, to collaborate.	Items for discussion are entered into the ALCM and this becomes the agenda. In Waterfall, this list would be referred to as an "issues log."	All members should at least be present at the start of this ceremony to find out if a topic impacts them.	Daily, 15 minutes long, immediately after the Daily Standup. *Comment:* Most texts do not call this activity out as a ceremony. However, it does seem very similar in nature to processes that bare the title of ceremony.

Comment: Ceremonies that support the iteration, and are explicitly tied to the iteration's cycle, should be scheduled immediately after a team determines the duration of its iterations. This way, all team members can plan to attend well in advance of the cyclically held ceremony.

Story Points are stored along with the other metadata in the related User Story. The main point here is that the estimate is being created by "relative sizing." No "hours" or "days" are used in this process. Remembering that human behavior is to hear a dollar value and stick to it, using Story Points removes this attachment to an early estimate as you cannot really assign a dollar value to something so arbitrary. However, with respect to Iteration capacity considerations, Story Points have proven to work just fine.

A word of warning. It would not be all that hard to map Story Point values to estimate hours. If you do this, you will corrupt the value of "relative" sizing and you could find yourself being locked into providing a premature, solid estimate.

A number that is needed to make Story Points work is called "Velocity." Velocity is the total number of Story Points that can be accepted in an Iteration by an AgileScrumTeam. This number is unique to each AgileScrumTeam and the AgileScrumTeam can change the Velocity from Iteration to Iteration. The team determines this number by taking a guess as to how many Story Points of work they can process in an Iteration. For example, I am writing this in early January. What we did with my AgileScrumTeam in December was to reduce our velocity significantly as many people were on long vacations around the holidays.

For example, let us say that one step in the project from Chapter 2 is to take off the tires of a car to install the devices that can start stinking if a car moves faster than 75 miles/hour. That seems pretty simple as a good mechanic can pull off tires in about 10 or less minutes. Compared to our Pivot User Story, I think that would qualify for a Story Point of 1. As for filling out all the paperwork and forms needed to find and use a race track for the car to go over the 75 miles/hour mark, that is no easier nor harder than any other user story; so I would give that the same value as the pivot User Story, a value of 8.

An obvious question is, how do hours ever fit in? Well, the User Stories that are small enough to be completed in one iteration, are further decomposed one last time, by the BuildTeam. This last decomposition results in "Tasks." Tasks are what the BuildTeam uses to complete work, and, hours or days are the time unit associated with those.

Burn Down Chart

A burn down chart shows how much of your available time you have used as a team, as compared to a line that assumes a constant use of hours, at the same level, each day.

To understand time in a project sense, you need to understand the two distinct terms **Effort** and **Duration**. Effort is a term from the classical project management community. It means how many hours that are actually spent working on task. Duration is a related term; it means how much time passes while working on an assigned task, whether the resource is actively engaged on task or not. For example, presume "Terri" is working on one task, on and off for 4 days. So:

- Under Duration time reporting, the 4 days would be included in the time she was working on the assigned task. This is the type of estimate used during Story Pointing.
- Under Effort driven time reporting, she would report only time on task. This is the type of estimate that is done when you are estimating at a Task level.

How to build a Burn Down Chart

Here are our assumptions:

- You are a ScrumMaster.
- There are three people on your team, and each starts with 80 estimated hours of actual on task work effort hours, across an iteration that lasts 2 weeks.
- All actual and estimated hours are effort hours, and are pulled from estimates entered onto tasks. (These estimates and actuals are supplied by the people doing the work.)
- The person doing the work supplied the initial estimate, and on a daily basis will supply an estimate of the work left to be done.

First, we shall use the above information to draw what I call the "Perfect Burn Down Line." This is the line that assumes that all work happens at a constant pace until all hours are used up when the Iteration ends.

- So at the start of the first iteration, we have 240 hours worth of work to do (80 * 3), that is, 80 hours times 3 people. This assumes they are on task from the minute they walk in the door, till the time they leave work 8 hours later.

- We have 10 business days in the iteration.
- We have 0 hours left of estimated hours at the end of the iteration.

This graph represents a perfect burn down. It is what I use to gauge performance against during an iteration:

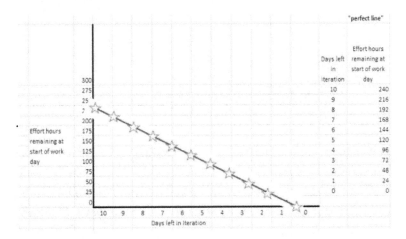

Comment: The above is the Perfect Burn Down Line. It is based on the Effort hours accepted into an iteration. The assumption is that a perfect Iteration would eat up and equal number of hours in a day, and there would be no hours available at the end of the Iteration.

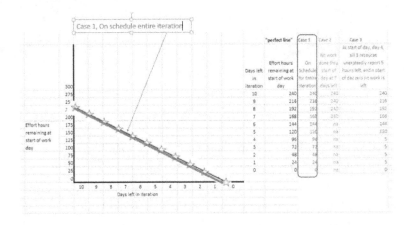

Comment: This is quite rare! This is the case where a team is on schedule for the entirety of the Iteration.

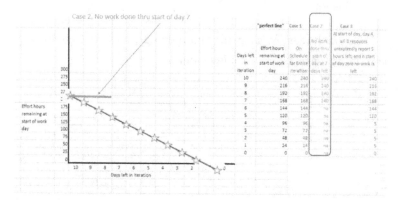

Comment: This means no one is working on the iteration. The ScrumMaster needs to talk to the BuildTeam!

Comment: When the work left is above the Perfect Burn Down Line, and all information is accurately reflected in the Burn Down Chart, this team is behind schedule.

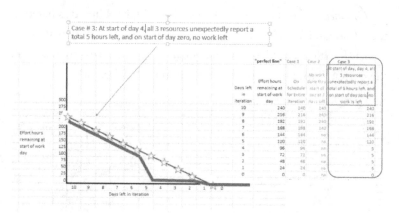

Comment: In Burn Down Charts, when the hours left to complete line is below the Perfect Burn Down Line, this means the team is ahead of schedule. At the start of day 4, it is apparent that the team is comfortably ahead of schedule. Were I ScrumMaster, I would find out why the sudden drop in effort hours took place. I would suspect the team did something brilliant to get so far ahead. Once out, if my guess was correct, I would share the success, of the AgileScrumTeam, widely.

Comment: When the work left line is below the perfect burn down line, and all information is accurately reflected in the Burn Down Chart, the team is ahead of schedule.

How this is used:

When I started a ScrumTeam in the middle of summer, I realized it was actually an accomplishment to have a working Burn Down chart to look at. About the middle of the second Iteration it was in good enough condition to start using it for its intended purpose. A working Burn Down Chart is a signal that the team is functioning well in terms of adopting the Agile Scrum Process as many items need to take place, correctly, for the Burn Down Chart to work well.

Where I use it is at the start of our official Daily Standup, I briefly show it, and call out anything that the Burn Down chart is showing. My current AgileScrumTeam is composed of AgileCoaches. The only issue we ever really have, which the burn down chart shows, is a slow start on iterations. But even that is improving over time.

With an ALCM, any executive who wants to invest a few minutes to understand how to use the ALCM to pull statuses can easily pull a status on any AgileScrumTeam. This means that all AgileScrumTeam members must keep their time information up to date, or it is only a matter of time before the ScrumMaster gets an unpleasant phone call.

A Warning

There is a special case of the Burn Down Chart that you should be aware of. Let us propose that there are only 2 days left of the iteration, up until now your team was on schedule, and then your team learns that a massive defect is discovered in the architecture you based your work effort on. In other words, there is now a sink-hole of time to invest, and no one was previously aware of the massive time investment. This would mean:

- this chart was fine until this point,
- the burn down chart was telling the stakeholder community that everything was in good shape,

- there was nothing to worry about, right up until there are just 2 days left.

Then on the next to last day of the iteration, the chart suddenly displays a huge disparity between planned and actual. Be aware that this chart can only display what is known, and reasonably expected. Meaning, just because a burn down chart paints a rosy picture for 80% of an iteration does NOT mean the last 20 percent will be easy-peasy.

An example was when we had 4 days left to our last iteration of the release, and then results from friendly user testing came in with 20 defects that needed to get fixed. That significantly changed our burn down chart, quite unexpectedly.

Summary

In summary, this chapter identified the minimum infrastructure necessary to have an AgileScrumTeam function. We covered Ceremonies, Story Points, and Burn Down charts. After a team is comfortable with these systems, progress in realizing the value of Agile Scrum should take place.

Knowledge Reinforcement

1. Assume that you are about to take a trip for pleasure to Madagascar. What is your Epic level User Story, and then break the Epic up into four smaller user stories which address that is needed.
2. If in the middle of an iteration it is discovered that a User Story is too large for a release, who should the DevelopmentTeam and/or TestTeam member notify?
3. Why is it important to put User Stories into the provided format?
4. There is a new project. Which member of the Agile Scrum Team is are most likely to bring the project to the AgileScrumTeam?
5. Who is most responsible for creating quality User Stories that relate directly to a project.
6. What is the last time that a team can say no to working a User Story that is in the wrong format, lacks clarity and has wrong or misleading metadata?

7. Class Discussion: If a ProductOwner is too busy to attend the team's Ceremonies, especially Backlog Grooming and Vision: what can be done to better engage the Product Owner? Please note, if you ever look at the calendar of a Product Owner, you will see that they are at back-to-back meetings all day. This is because these people are a critical asset to the performing organization as a whole.

8. (Class discussion) Assume that you are training a new member of a team; the new and improved ScrumMaster! She wants to make a list of everything she should learn to be effective when she takes over in 3 weeks. What would you recommend being on the list? How can you use this list in your day-to-day operations with your AgileScrumTeam.

9. After a few years of using Agile Scrum, you are pretty sure you can map Story Point numbers to hours. Would this be a good thing?

10. Assume the following:

Iteration	Story Point Value Completed in Iteration
2	10
3	25
4	31
5	29
6	30

What would you pick as the Velocity going forward, and why? (*comment*: there are many potential correct answers to this).

11. A contractor wants to use Story Points in a variable cost contract to determine cost to you. That is, as the AgileScrumTeam you are thinking about hiring estimates Story Points, and then completes Story Pointed User Stories, you then get charged per Story Point completed. Is this a good idea for you? Why or why not?

12. Given the three Burn Down Charts below, which Agile ScrumTeam needs the most help right now? Assume both charts are up-to-date.

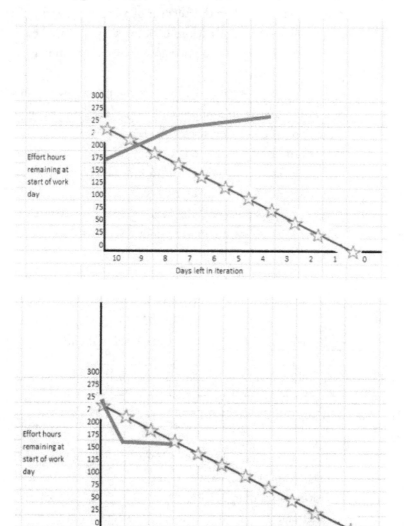

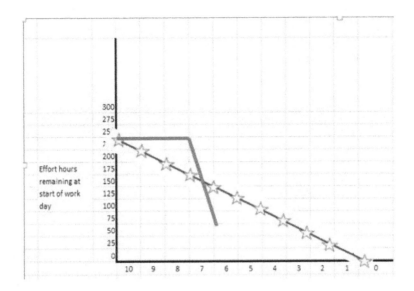

CHAPTER 4

The Agile Scrum Team

"Coming together is a beginning. Keeping together is progress. Working together is success!"

Henry Ford

Chapter Purpose

As a current and former leader of many teams, across many years
I want to explain the Agile "team" concept
So that people can achieve the synergy which only that of team can bring to a project.

In this chapter, I elaborate on activities performed by Agile Scrum teams, that result in high performance. That is, delivering more of the value-adding "ask" from the ProductOwner, team empowerment, and delivering value to the business quickly.

The AgileScrumTeam's Composition

There are three major parts to an Agile scrum team; ProductOwner, BuildTeam, and ScrumMaster. In this book, we have split the BuildTeam into two teams—DevelopmentTeam and TestTeam. This was done to increase readability. Please see the chart below for a visual reference to this...

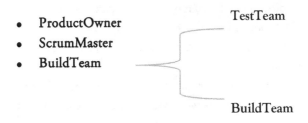

- **ProductOwner**
- **ScrumMaster**
- **BuildTeam**

TestTeam

BuildTeam

An AgileScrumTeam has five to nine people. Both the Product Owner and ScrumMaster play a leadership role. The ProductOwner sets the strategic (longer term) direction, and the ScrumMaster's role is more immediate (i.e., tactical). As for where the term Scrum Comes from, it is from a game that is popular in Europe, called rugby.

In rugby, at some points in the game, a battle of two scrums takes place for a ball. That is, each scrum of eight people fights to gain possession of the ball. They communicate primarily by body movement as they have their arms around each other in an interlocking style. And, each member of the scrum applies their force to drive the other team back. I assume the reason the name stuck was because metaphorically there is a close relationship between a rugby scrum and what our AgileScrumTeam does. Please find below a description of each part of the AgileScrumTeam. Then, once you have a good idea about what the Agile Scrum Team does, there will be some tricks and tips shared that can make an AgileScumTeam even more effective.

ScrumMaster

One of the two leadership roles on an AgileScrum to the team is that of a ScrumMaster. In general, they monitor the adoption of Agile Scrum adoption, and implement corrective teaching when necessary. Through effective listening, and occasionally detective work, they identify when team members are experiencing roadblocks, and make sure the right resources are brought to bear to elevate issues. Or if that does not work, they fix it themselves. They are a leader, who is there to *serve* and guide. They do not assign work; rather the team members request work to do. And, they also manage the day-to-day details to make sure the iterations run smoothly. Some specific roles they perform are:

- Be a champion of Agile who makes sure the agile process runs smoothly and all Ceremonies are executed correctly.
- Make sure Ceremonies are scheduled and carried out.
- Leads some Ceremonies (see the Ceremony section in a previous chapter).
- Is a participant in in the Scrum-of-Scrum ceremonies (This is where co-dependencies between teams are discussed, and joint plans are created to keep teams in sync.).

- They are a Champion for team to ensure they work at a "sustainable pace."
- Protect the team from outside distractions like politics, etc.
- Ensure the team looks professional at Demos through effective scheduling of topics and holding Demo planning meetings (Demos are a great time to impress your paying client!).
- They attend and/or lead any ceremony they are expected at, and show up on time, and prepared.
- In a crisis, can switch quickly in and out of an autocratic leadership style based on the immediacy or tedium of a requested task.
- Has a passion for seeing their team members being effective.
- Keeps an eye on Opportunity Cost as it relates to new User Stories being accepted into an iteration. That is, they confirm that new User Stories do not impede User Stories of a higher priority, and, the ProductOwner understands any necessary tradeoffs before a User Story is accepted.

The above list is long, and rather difficult to digest. So, let me make it a bit easier. People are largely defined by their expected behaviors. Here is a diagram that should help put all these into a context, and thus make the information more actionable:

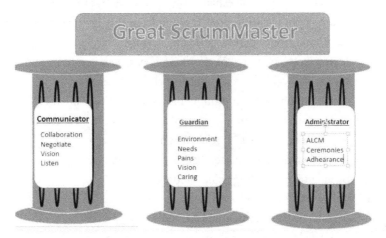

As implied by the diagram above, the three most important behaviors of great ScrumMasters are;

- *Understanding*: They understand the technical environment. This means that when ScrumTeam members need help, the ScrumMaster has the background to engage on behalf of the team. They are also cognizant of the needs that the team has. For example, the TestTeam may need faster download speeds, smarter computers, etc. Since the ScrumMasters understand the need, they are active in trying to meet it. They are also understanding of the political environment. When they do not have the direct authority to complete a task, they know who to go to in order to achieve resolution. One special trait is that they understand when to step in to help, and when to step back and let the team members grow. They also have a keen sense of what User Stories are in scope of the application and business, that is, they understand the organizational vision, and the role their application fills in supporting that vision.
- *Communicator*: They are skilled at sending and receiving messages using various mediums. One item that truly separates the average ScrumMaster from the best is making the time to create a "social contract" and storing it for all to see. This has in it the explanation of how the team is to run, and processes it will follow. It has links to any document the team might find useful. It also has a clause that team members are *to treat each other with dignity and respect*. One more thing they do exceptionally well is encourage collaboration between team members by ensuring varied communication channels are available and used by the team. They make sure that informal communications take place regularly among team members and often employ by playing team building games (more on this below).
- *Adherence*: The ALCM takes on a life of its own after using it for a while. A well-chosen ALCM will guide you to entering in the needed data; mostly statuses and metadata for User Stories. But, it is my experience that the people on

the DevelopmentTeam tend not to keep this up to date. Unfortunately for the ScrumMaster a well set up ALCM drives transparency. Meaning that when your friends on the DevelopmentTeam do not enter actual hours, it looks like your efforts are behind schedule. Therefore, to keep your stakeholders happy, you need to stay after your delinquent team members to keep the ALCM up to date. One way to do this is to call out the update status just before your Daily Standup starts. The great ScrumMasters are very sure to hold all Ceremonies that are needed, and *never* cancel the Daily Standup; this ensures team members stay in the habit of showing up.

ProductOwner

This is the primary person who asks for change and new functionality relating to the current project or program by adding User Stories to the Backlog. They:

- are very cognizant of the business and end user(s) of the application.
- work with the other members of the AgileScrumTeam to create and capture ideas (during Vision ceremonies) as User Stories.
- prioritize User Stories.
- improve User Stories during Backlog Grooming Ceremonies.
- approve work products when they are ready, and view the combination of all work products in a Demo.
- they alone approve User Stories as time goes on as the work completes, and occasionally approve User Stories during the Demo.

It is essential to team success that the ProductOwner attend any ceremony they are expected at, show up on time, and be prepared. They should make themselves available for consultations. The expectations of this person should be spelled out in writing at the start of the effort because these people tend to be hard to reach.

DevelopmentTeam and the TestTeam
(Aka. The BuildTeam)

The BuildTeam is composed of the DevelopmentTeam, the TestTeam, and possibly a part-time architect. On a high-performing AgileScrumTeam, roles between Developers and Testers are blurred as AgileScrumTeams strive for role interchangeability. The AgileScrumTeam relies on the BuildTeam to:

- Help during backlog grooming to decompose User Stories
- To write Tasks. Tasks have detail design, check lists, and similar items in them. They are subordinate to all User Stories.
- Keep the ALCM fields up to date with status, actuals, etc.
- Create the test conditions and/or acceptance criteria, and store them in the appropriate User Story and/or task
- Participate heavily in the creation of a social contract (the Social Contract is covered earlier in this chapter)
- Assist the when they create high-level estimates called Story Points (discussed later in this chapter)
- Ask the Product Owner for approval on completed work products
- Attend Ceremonies as expected, and participate as expected
- Request work and commit to completing it during an iteration, while at the iteration planning ceremony.
- Attend any ceremony they are expected at, and show up on time and prepared

Joining a Preexisting Agile Scrum Team

When I was a new, first-time ScrumMaster, I tended to manage work and not actually participate. What I came to realize was that I did not speak the language the team was speaking. Well before being a Scrum-Master, I had been a top-rated analyst (designer/coder/tester), but as I was on a state of the art knowledge repository, I had a lot to learn. What I learned most of all was that this team had their own language that was a composite of industry terms, and a few terms I only heard on the team. The process I eventually used to understand the everyday jargon of the team was to write down every term the team used, and get a description through one of three ways:

- Using Wikipedia, Google, Bing, books or similar sources
- The assistance of my friends both on the team and outside the team.
- Digging into the documentation the team had

Then there are three important things to keep in mind. First, developers are usually very happy to explain their work *once*. But, don not ask them the same question twice. They seem to take this as a big affront. Second, when you are collecting all the terms, find a way to double check your work, and if it is accurate, post it in a common area so others can use it. I suggest checking your answers because on a few instances, people have unwittingly shared partial or inaccurate information with me. Though this was not intentional, but, what it showed me was there was indeed a reason to document all the terms.

The other big activity that I did was to update the process map of the application. As AgileScrum teams are not fond of documentation, it was hard to find a skeleton to start with, and then easy to find areas that needed to be updated. I saved all this knowledge into a common location too for others to learn from it.

From my perspective, what was interesting was that since I had invested time learning about the day-to-day work, and I now understood the conversations at the various ceremonies, the team welcomed me in. I can say this as they started valuing my opinions, and when crisis mode happened they welcomed my lead.

Trust

Trust is when you can expect a person to do the right thing when no one is looking, and do even better when they know that someone is depending on them. The best way to begin to establish trust on an Agile ScrumTeam is to prove that you are invested into the team. Here are some ideas on establishing that you are in it for the long haul. For those of you who have read Warren Bennis's *On Becoming a Leader (2003)*, you will recognize the format of the below information. That is, a bad trait is shared first on each line, and then a desired contra behavior:

- Remaining clueless about the team you just joined versus investing one's self to understand the necessary functions
- Committing and not performing versus taking on tasks, and successfully delivering on time
- Doing business the same old way versus taking actions requested at recent Retrospectives
- Ignoring work that others will be held accountable for versus updating the ALCM daily?
- Merely attending ceremonies versus being an active participant
- Ignoring programming standards versus coding correctly and mechanically confirming standards are adhered to.
- Being the ProductOwner who is just too busy for the team versus the ProductOwner who makes time to meet the BuildTeam's needs
- Being late to, or missing ceremonies versus being ready and on time for ceremonies.
- Glossing over issues versus seeking out issues and targeting them for resolution.

In summary, the way to establish trust is to meet the expectations of the AgileScrumTeam as the Agile Scrum Methodology has been shown so far in this book.

Clear Expectations:

When one is on a team, it can be difficult to understand what the culture expects. It is the responsibility of the ScrumMaster to lead the team in creating a social contract. What a social contract does is establishes the expectations that team members will expect from each other. Here are some ideas for your social contract:

- A general statement of conduct that looks something like this: *All team members are to be treated with dignity and respect. This includes listening to all team members, especially when their opinions differ from that of the majority.*

- Team members are to learn how to leverage each other's talents for the good of the team. I do recommend having all team members post their resumes I a common location. This is essential in understanding who knows what.
- What the duration of the Agile Scrum Cycle is
- When in the Agile Scrum Cycle, what the various cycle-dependent ceremonies will be
- What the time expectations are for the ProductOwner
- Adherence to Agile Scrum in all aspects of building and modifying the Product Backlog
- Ability to attend the Retrospective, and especially the Demonstration ceremonies
- The process to update the Social Agreement. That is, who approves any proposed changes. And what percent of the approvers need to approve changes to the agreement.
- The standards that the DevelopmentTeam will be guided by
- For international teams, when will they meet to minimize the discomfort of time zone differences, to the greatest extent on all participants?
- A commitment from the ProductOwner to respect the team's velocity
- When the TestTeam will begin creating test cases
- How teams are to stay in constant communication
- What information flows to whom and how
- Important links to essential documents
- What is expected from a User Story before the team will consider accepting it into an iteration. This is also called the definition of "Ready."
- The definition of "Done" and "Done–Done"

The main idea here is that if team members are aware upfront what their responsibilities are, it is more likely they will perform as desired. Also, should someone choose to be a nonperformer on the team, the Social Contract can be a fair way of assessing the individual's history of meeting commitments.

Team Building:

Team building is a method used to increase trust and communication amongst team members through artificially amplifying the intensity and duration of collaboration across a relatively short duration of time. The typical team-building method is to do a shared highly interactive activity. My favorite team-building exercise is when they are first meeting each other using video conferencing for each person to share an avatar of themselves. It is amazing to see all the varied interpretations of avatar. An avatar is supposed to be a character of a person, but sometimes I see self-image art like golf clubs. The odd responses to the request usually bring a smile to all participants. There are many other ways for teams to break the ice on an ongoing pattern. For example, one boss I had brought in an Italian Ice cart, and a catered lunch on Wednesdays! One recent trend I am seeing is to put people with like jobs into the same room. This is an easy way to foster communication and collaboration.

In short, there are three things that must be in place to build teams:

- A social contract, so everyone is on the same page
- A ScrumMaster and Product owner who are committed to the Agile Scrum process
- Team-building activities to keep the team acting as a unit

Now, here is something interesting about Avatars; they sometimes tell you what the self-image is of the person drawing it. If you can pick up on this, you have one more clue how to effectively collaborate with the person.

A word of caution. There are charity events that sound like team building opportunities where you get to paint, rake mulch, and clean up disgusting parks. These activities are fine as a giveback, but it is my experience that they have limited value as team building. Rather, what I try to do is pair the team's skills with a real live issue. For example, have the team work in a high-school for a day, and teach students what it is like to do software development. Or, maybe have the entire team gather to fix an IT business problem of a charity. The idea here is unlike those paint-the-walls activities, if you can leverage your team's core competence, you can strengthen the bonds of your team members, and make a meaningful impact on people's lives. I have personally done Junior Achievement several times. Each time I felt like I did something note-worthy because while I am there I get to teach a business skill. For a giveback like this, one would have to have a fun follow-up for the team so that they can interact and share their day's events.

Summary

In this chapter, we learned about teams, and the structure of teams in the Agile Scrum Environment. This is important as the team must be organized in order to be top-performing with respect to consistently meeting the "asks" of the business.

References

Bennis, W.G. 2003. *On Becoming a Leader*. Cambridge, MA: Perseus Publishing.

CHAPTER 5

A Look at Risk from Classical Project Management

"By failing to prepare, you are preparing to fail."

Ben Franklin

Chapter Purpose

As an Agile Scrum practitioner and coach,
I want to identify and share a part of Classical Project Management
So that Agile practitioners can become even more effective.

It amazes me that the role of risk seems not to be a main concern in Agile Scrum. The reason AgileScrumTeams seem to spend so little time on risk is that Agile Scrum virtually addresses risk by having demos, limiting the duration of time activities can be worked on (iterations) before Product Owners evaluate results, and doing risky User Stories first. Realistically, unless the team is making a concerted effort to address risk, unanticipated events will likely occur more often, and with greater impact. Below, please find a quick introduction to Risk should you choose to adopt risk management in your day-to-day AgileScrumTeam efforts.

Introduction to Risk Management

Risk is the prospect that there could be a difference between what is hoped for and what actually happens. The outcome could be either more negative than projected, or positive. As a practical matter, negative risks tend to get more attention. *The main idea is that you want a plan in place as soon as a potential event is uncovered,* so that should the event manifest itself you are more able to successfully respond to it.

One question is where to store this information related to Risk. Storing risk information in the ALCM is a logical place. I would expect that an ALCM allows for easy access to risks and related metadata as if the risks related to a single User Story, and, the ALCM should allow for entire list of risks so they can be viewed at a project level.

The idea of storing risks and related data on one place is nothing new; in classical project management, they call it a Risk Register.

To continue, there are valuable benefits from assessing risks in your project. For example:

- If you do a good job at risk planning, you will be more prepared than if you did nothing.
- If something comes up out of nowhere and there is a formal investigation, you can point to your formal processes and how effectively you planned, despite the result.
- Working with risk can help teach the people in your organization critical thinking and value-based reasoning.
- This is a good way for teams to learn collaboration, and learn more about their own applications as they start to understand process vulnerabilities, and address them.

Here is a process that has worked for me to address Risk:

Input:

- Any assumptions relating to the project or specific User Stories
- All User Stories in the User Story backlog that will likely get worked on
- Feedback from expert consultation
- History from previous, similar efforts
- When available, any pertinent company records
- Gut feel/intuition

Process:

1. Create a list of known risk events. There are several methods to do this:
   1.1 *Basic Method*: Leverage the inputs to identify Risks that are obvious to the AgileScrumTeam.

1.2 *Brain storming:* Brain storming is a well-documented way for team members to collaborate. This is similar to crowd sourcing.

1.3 *Examining the infrastructure with respect to:*

   1.3.1   The current architecture

   1.3.2   *How programs interact with each other with in the context of the application*

   1.3.3   *Inter-relationships with other applications*

   1.3.4   *Ability to discover defects and react to them (Detectability)*

   1.3.5   *How information is transmitted and securely stored*

   1.3.6   *Etc.*

1.4 *Modified Fishbone* (This assumes that you are familiar with fishbone. If not, this is well spelled out on the web.)

As a risk-assessment tactic, a modified fishbone can be used to assist in understanding the terrain and identifying potential issues well before the code is written. Pretend that when you go into production, and then the deployment was a "total failure." The words "Total failure" is entered in the head the fish. Then the team, with a little imagination, and a few assumptions, is asked to do the Fishbone process as if a real crisis happened. Risks should be captured by a scribe.

2.   Once risks are detected, and then entered into the ALCM, here are some examples of metadata that can be included as metadata for risks when described on the Risk Log. Immediately following the description of the metadata will be an example based on the risk potential of drilling a hole into electrical wires that are inside of the walls we are putting dry wall on. These examples will be within brackets and also in italics:

2.1 Impact 1–5: 5 = highest impact *{This is potentially life threatening, therefore an impact of 5 seems appropriate}*

2.2 Probability 1–5: 5= highest impact *{this seems to rarely happen as dry wall installers know to watch out for this so a probability of 2 will be assigned to it}*

2.3 Priority (Scale 1–25: Impact multiplied by Probability) *{an impact of 5 multiplied by a probability of 2 gives us a priority of "10"}*

2.4 If "scale" is greater than your risk tolerance level:

2.4.1 then who "owns" it ("X" is selected by the organization based on their level of risk aversion) *{I would assign the activity of NOT drilling into electrical wires to the dry wall installers}*

2.4.2 Quantitative assessment of risk (e.g., NPV/EMV) *{Though not an NPV analysis, the cost could easily be the cost of covering law suits by people who could get hurt in a potential fire caused by drilling electrical wires. Another cost is the cost of potentially rebuilding the home from scratch.}*

2.4.3 Qualitative assessment of risk *{If workers are hurt, it could take a while to find competent dry wall people to replace them.}*

2.4.4 Trigger event(s) {A trigger event is someone drilling a hole into the dry wall to affix it to the wall and accidentally drilling into electrical wires}

2.4.5 Warning signs *{Some warning signs can include a pop of a circuit breaker, a smoke smell, etc.}*

2.4.6 How to monitor for a risk event *{One could take pictures of the area before drywall is applied and confirm no drilling takes place near wires within the walls.}*

2.4.7 Planned response:

2.4.7.1 Transfer: like insurance, transfer the risk to someone else (realistically, this is very difficult to do in an IT area) *{Buying insurance to protect from workers suing and potential damage to the home would be a good example of transferring risk to an insurance company.}*

2.4.7.2 Avoid: Once the trigger events for a risk are observed, identify how to make those trigger events never take place, or reduce the chance of them occurring *{As mentioned above, pictures can be taken as to where wires are hiding in walls. Not drilling where known wires are should reduce the probability of an adverse outcome.}*

2.4.7.3 Accept the risk as in just let it happen (be especially sure to document this type of risk response, and share your findings with your executive stakeholders for input and approval). *{Though a very bad idea, workers could just ignore the risk and drill away. Again, this would be a very bad idea.}*

2.4.7.4 Mitigating is actually implementing a plan to address a risk (what is nice about this is you actually address the risk head on. But keep an eye on any actual backup process as they tend to decay with time). *{On the day that drywall is put up, close visual inspection can take place to identify the location of wires. Also, sensitive metal detectors could be used to find any hidden wires. All information would be supplied to the dry wall workers. Also, several fire extinguishers are placed near where the dry wall workers will be working. Also, circuit breakers could be tested to make sure they would pop if danger was detected. Giving classes to the drywall installers on safety procedures could also prove helpful. Or, walls could be wired AFTER the drywall is up.}*

2.4.8 What risks are associated with making this change? *{Addressing a risk will likely cause other risks. In this case, trained drywall specialists may resent being told what to do.}*

2.4.9 What stakeholders need to know about this possibility, and if it takes place, who needs to be notified. *{The drywallers need to be made aware of this possibility; so if it happens, they are better able to address the situation. Also, if smoke is smelled, the calling fire fighters to the scene may be appropriate.}*

(The above was adopted from a previous work of the author, © 2013, and is used with permission.)

Output:

1. The filled-out risk register.
2. User Stories that are coupled with a risk are to be:
   a. Specifically pointed to by the risk register
   b. The User Story must point to its relevant risks on the user story.
3. A decision on how to address risk, plus a User Story is to be placed on the backlog to make it actionable.

Summary

It is my belief based on years of managing projects that if one prepares for risk events, then one is much more capable of dealing with them when the time comes. In this chapter, a clear method of dealing with risk and effectively managing it has been shared.

Knowledge Expansion

1. For a project you are working on, use the process indicated above to address three risk events.
2. Create an argument for the handling of one of your risks identified above if the team wants to ignore a risk.

Glossary

As an author

I want to: define the Agile terms used in these chapters, and other terms that may also need definition.

So that: as the reader absorbs the material, it is more easy to create a mental picture as to what is being discussed.

Agile Coach: An Agile evangelist whose role is to guide AgileScrumTeams in the correct use of Agile within an organization.

Acceptance Criteria: This is the list of new ProductOwner expectations as they relate to a single User Story.

Agile Life Cycle Management tool (ALCM): All information relevant to the project is stored on this software tool. For example, it houses User Stories and their metadata. These can typically generate custom reports which provide transparency.

AgileScrumTeam: This is composed of the ProductOwner, the BuildTeam, and the ScrumMaster. These teams have between five and nine members and stay together for a very long time.

ALCM: See Agile Life Cycle Management tool.

Backlog: This is the repository where User Stories are placed before they are selected to be worked on. Once a User Story on the Backlog is groomed, it can be requested by a team member to be worked on. When a User Story is selected to be worked on, it is moved to the Iteration-Backlog.

Backlog Grooming (this is a Ceremony): The process of massaging User Stories in the Backlog in order to make sure User Stories in the Backlog are the correct format for a User Story. The people attending the Backlog Grooming Ceremony must also determine if all needed information is supplied within the User Story so they can mark a User Story Ready for being considered for a candidate for Iteration Planning. If a User Story is too big to fit in an Iteration, it is decomposed/broken-up into smaller User Stories.

BuildTeam: This is composed of the DevelopmentTeam and the TestTeam.

Burn down Chart: This is a graph that shows the difference between how many hours the team has used and how many hours the team should have burned up based on daily velocity, where in this case, velocity is expressed in hours. Hours spent on a task are to be updated daily in the ALCM in order to have this chart be current for discussion at the daily standup. This chart can be expressed in hours, Story Points, or both.

Classic Project Management: Synonymous with "Waterfall." Please see "Waterfall" in this glossary.

Daily Standup (this is a Ceremony): A ceremony in which all team members attend each working day. Four questions are to be answered: (1) What have you done since the last daily standup? (2)What have you planned before the next standup? (3) Do you have any impediments? and (4) Did you update the ALCM? This meeting appears to be constructed to allow peer pressure to encourage each person on the AgileScrumTeam to work at a sustainable, optimal pace.

Deliverable: A work product that is known to satisfy all relevant requirements, acceptance criteria, and test cases.

Done: This term is to be defined by the AgileScrumTeam based on its processes, environment, and needs. In general, it means that the ProductOwner has approved the story and it has been reviewed during a Demo. (Please see "Done–Done" in this glossary).

Done–Done: This term is to be defined by the AgileScrumTeam based on its processes, environment, and needs. The definition the team uses is to be stored in the Social Contract, which is stored in the ALCM. In general, a "Done–Done" User Story has been deployed into the production environment and is ready for the end user to use in day-to-day processes.

Demo (a ceremony): Slang for the ceremony called "Demonstration." See "Demonstration."

Demonstration (a ceremony): The work product relating to all User Stories that have completed in the current iteration are celebrated in the presence of the ProductOwner. Occasionally, a User Story is approved during the Demonstration, but this is to be avoided.

Detectability: The ability to identify a defect which is present.

DevelopmentTeam: These are the people who create the working code. They typically do unit testing, and run any code validation software. This does not include those who are dedicated to testing.

Duration: The number of calendar working days a task takes to get done. This includes breaks, idle time etc. For example, if a human resource spends 4.5 hours on a task across 3 days, then the duration is 3 days. Also see "effort hours."

General Contractor: The person is in charge of a construction project. In this text, this is the same as a ScrumMaster or a project manager.

Grooming: The activities that take place during a Backlog Grooming Ceremony.

Effort Hours: Hours spent specifically on a task.

Epic Level User Story: Reveals the objective of the project to be undertaken by the AgileScrumTeam. These are decomposed to provide better meaning and direction to the BuildTeam.

Iteration: A time period, typically 2 to 4 weeks long, during which committed User Stories are completed.

Iteration Backlog: This is where User Stories originally located in the Backlog are moved to when they are to be worked on during the upcoming Iteration.

Iteration Planning (a ceremony): If the metadata on a User Story in the backlog is sufficient, and it has the highest priority, and a BuildTeam member asks to work on it, then it is moved to the Iteration Backlog. Once on the Iteration Backlog, the work effort is considered to be committed work for the current Iteration.

Methodology: A process which guides a development team as it creates a work product.

Metadata: Data that further defines other data. For example, say you own 20 clothes-washers. On a database, you may keep data about each of your clothes-washers like hours out of service per month, capacity of the machine, gallons of water per use, and money collected per day etc.

Opportunity Cost: Occasionally, selecting one course of action precludes taking up other activities. The activities you can no longer take action on are the "cost" in opportunity cost.

Parking Lot (a ceremony): This ceremony immediately follows the Daily Standup. All pressing issues are to be brought up and discussed until they are resolved or actionable. It is 15 minutes long; so people have to choose carefully what to talk about and how long they talk for. Items that do not fit into the 15-minute time slot can be moved to their own meeting forum later in the near future (Comment: most texts do not refer to the Parking Lot as a ceremony yet).

Pivot User Story: The establishment of a User Story that is of average size. When Story Pointing, all items that undergo Story Point are given an estimate relative to this User Story.

ProductOwner: The person who:

- Works to understand the needs, pains, and desires of the ultimate consumer of the value of an application.
- Expresses the needs of this community in words that are in User Story format.
- Populates most User Stories on to the Backlog.
- Prioritizes User Stories on the Backlog.
- Accepts the Work-Product that is created based on User Story's "ask."
- Assists in creating Acceptance Criteria and Test Cases.
- Answers questions relating to any aspect of a User Story.

Project: A nonrepetitive, well-defined, time-boxed, and finite effort to meet the documented needs of a stakeholder community and is unique to the performing organization (This definition is from an unpublished work of Brian Vanderjack's © 2007, used with permission).

Project Charter: Identifies the high-level deliverable of a project. It is signed by an executive with enough powers to:

- Protect the project team from external adversity and company politics.
- Push-needed initiatives related to the project.
- Be a friendly escalation point when a team has an issue it cannot react to.
- Maintain interest in the effort with other vitally needed executives.
- Keep track of project via reports supplied by the ScrumMaster project manager.
- Understand what the organization actually needs to get done.

It is to have enough information to start and keep the project going, but not so much that it proves to be an obstacle. The Epic User Story should directly flow from this document.

Ready: This is a flag (AKA indicator) on each User Story in the ALCM. Its presence indicates a User Story that has been successfully groomed, and it is "ready" to be selected into an Iteration.

Requirement: A description of a feature, function, or process related to an application. Typically these are grouped together in a meaningful narrative called a "requirements document."

Retrospective (an Agile Ceremony): It is a formal meeting scheduled at the end of each Iteration. All members of the AgileScrumTeam meet together and formally determine what went well and what did not go so good during the past Iteration. If the team agrees to try to fix an issue shared during a retrospective, then a User Story is to be created to ensure that the item is not forgotten.

Story Point: An early estimate applied to a User Story that is simply a representation of relative size. Typically the estimate is based on a simplified Fibonacci Sequence (1,2,3,5,8,13,21...) or tee-shirt size (XS, S, M, L, XL). Also see Velocity.

Task: A special case of the User Story. It is what the developers and testers create to support their specific work. It is the decomposition of a User Story, and it is not decomposed by itself. This is where effort hours—that is, hours-on-task—are logged. This entity does not necessarily follow the User Story format.

Team Building: A method used to increase trust, communication, and productivity amongst team members through artificially amplifying the intensity and duration of collaboration on a predefined activity across a relatively short duration of time. The typical team building method is to perform a shared activity.

Test Plans: A description of one or more input values or conditions into a program, application, or system. The input(s) trigger(s) a behavior. This is the description of the input(s) and the expected behavior(s).

Time-Box: When a team is committed to starting and ending an activity at an agreed-upon time.

User: The ultimate customer(s) of the functionality of the computer application. They are typically the ones whose wants and needs are addressed by the ProductOwner writing User Stories.

User Story: A statement that is very similar to a requirement. It is written in this format: "As a," "I want," and "So that." User Stories are prioritized and reside in the "Backlog" or "Iteration Backlog." Metadata associated with the User Story also includes release, need-by data, who has ownership etc.

User Story Backlog: See "Backlog."

Velocity: The total number of Story Points that an AgileScrumTeam agrees to work on during an Iteration while maintaining a sustainable pace.

Vision: A view of the future as held by the leader(s) of an organization. When correctly employed, all assets of the company are to be in full support of advancing the cause.

Visioning: The process of turning User-Needs/Requirements into User Stories for immediate placement on the Backlog. If the priority is high enough, the User Stories will be moved to an Iteration Backlog. When first entered into the Backlog, they are neither sized nor prioritized. Little or no metadata will be present when entered.

Vision Meeting (a ceremony): This ceremony can take place at any time, and as often as is necessary, to capture wants and needs in the form of User Stories. When there is enough known about the request to build a User Story, a new entry is placed on the backlog.

Waterfall: This is the predecessor of AgileScrum. It is characterized by a predominantly linear approach to completing projects.

Work Breakdown Structure (WBS): Looks like an organization chart or an outline. When in an organization-chart format, the top node identifies the project objective. The project objective is repeatedly decomposed into smaller project objectives. The "terminal nodes of a WBS" is the work package; these are what a project manager manages too. There can be many levels in a WBS. Work packages are the most narrowly defined items on the WBS, and they inhabit the lowest, most detailed level.

Work-product: It is the result of an effort to meet a requirement.

Index

OTHER TITLES IN THE PORTFOLIO AND PROJECT MANAGEMENT COLLECTION

Timothy Kloppenborg, Editor

- *Strategic Leadership of Portfolio and Project Management* by Timothy J. Kloppenborg (Xavier University and Laurence J. Laning)
- *Project Strategy and Strategic Portfolio Management: A Primer* by William H. A. Johnson (Pennsylvania State University) and Diane Parente (Pennsylvania State University)
- *The Power of Design-Build: A Guide to Effective Design-Build Project Delivery Using the SAFEDB-Methodology* by Sherif Hashem
- *Information Systems Project Management* by David Olson (University of Nebraska)
- *Leveraging Business Analysis for Project Success* by Vicki James
- *Project Portfolio Management: A Model for Improved Decision-Making* by Clive Enoch
- *Project Management Essentials* by Kathryn Wells and Timothy J. Kloppenborg

Business Expert Press has over 30 collections in business subjects such as finance, marketing strategy, sustainability, public relations, economics, accounting, corporate communications, and many others. For more information about all our collections, please visit www. businessexpertpress.com/collections.

Announcing the Business Expert Press Digital Library

Concise e-books business students need for classroom and research

This book can also be purchased in an e-book collection by your library as

- a one-time purchase,
- that is owned forever,
- allows for simultaneous readers,
- has no restrictions on printing, and
- can be downloaded as PDFs from within the library community.

Our digital library collections are a great solution to beat the rising cost of textbooks. e-books can be loaded into their course management systems or onto students' e-book readers. The **Business Expert Press** digital libraries are very affordable, with no obligation to buy in future years. For more information, please visit **www.businessexpertpress.com/librarians.** To set up a trail in the United States, please contact sales@businessexpertpress.com.